Imagine! 1

W9-BXW-061

Robbers at the Museum

By Paul Shipton

Illustrated by Fabiano Fiorin

Activities by Hannah Fish

Contents

OXFORD
UNIVERSITY PRESS

Ben
Rosie's brother

Rosie
Ben's sister

Grandpa

Clunk
Grandpa's robot

Bill
Grandpa's friend,
a museum guard

Now let's read about
Robbers at the Museum!

Rosie is painting a picture at the table.

Ben looks at the picture. 'It's nice,' he says. 'What is it? Is it a horse?'

'No, it isn't!' says Rosie.

Ben looks at the picture again. 'Is it a cow?' he asks.

'No!' says Rosie. 'It's a cat!'

She looks at her picture. 'I'm not good at art,' she says. 'I don't want to paint now.'

I'm not good at art.

Go to page 20 for activities.

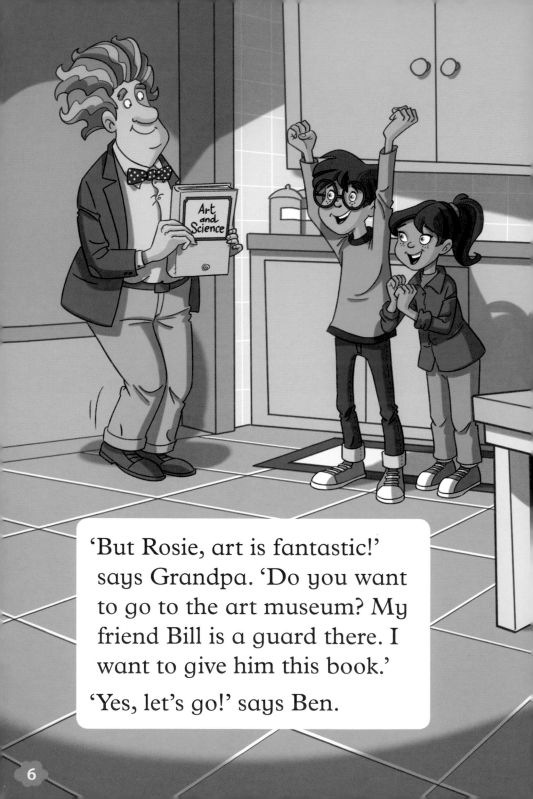

'But Rosie, art is fantastic!' says Grandpa. 'Do you want to go to the art museum? My friend Bill is a guard there. I want to give him this book.'

'Yes, let's go!' says Ben.

Grandpa's robot, Clunk, drives the van to the art museum.

Grandpa sees his friend.

'Meet my friend Bill,' says Grandpa to the children.

'Nice to meet you,' say Ben and Rosie.

Nice to meet you.

Go to page 21 for activities.

'I want to talk to your grandfather about this book,' says Bill to Ben and Rosie. 'You can look at the museum.'

Clunk goes with Ben and Rosie.

'Do you like art, Clunk?' asks Ben.

'I don't know,' says Clunk.

Do you like art, Clunk?

Ben points at a blue vase. 'Look at this vase,' he says. 'It's very old.'

Clunk doesn't like the vase.

'Do you like these statues?' asks Rosie.

Clunk doesn't like the statues.

Look at this vase.

→ Go to page 22 for activities.

Ben points at a big picture. 'I like the colors in this picture,' he says.

'I like this picture,' says Clunk. 'It's my favorite.'

'That isn't a picture, Clunk,' says Rosie. 'That's a museum sign!'

I like this picture.

Ben stops. 'Listen!' he says. 'Can you hear people?'

'Yes, I can,' says Rosie. 'Who is it?'

'I don't know,' says Ben. He points at a window. 'Look! There's a man at the window.'

→ Go to page 23 for activities.

Two men in black clothes are at the window.

'They're robbers!' says Ben. 'They want to steal the art!'

'Quick, run!' says Rosie.

But there isn't a door close to the children.

They're robbers!

'I have an idea!' says Ben. 'Quick! Come to these statues!'

They stand next to the statues.

'Now don't talk and don't move!' says Ben.

 Go to page 24 for activities.

 13

The two robbers are in the museum now. One of them has the blue vase in his hands.

'What do you want to steal?' he asks.

His friend points a flashlight at some pictures.

'Let's see,' he says.

'I want to steal a statue,' says the robber with the vase.

His friend looks at the statues. Then he looks at the children and Clunk.

'I don't like this little statue,' he says. 'It's ugly!'

It's ugly!

Go to page 25 for activities.

'I am not ugly!' says Clunk.

'The statues can talk!' says the robber with the vase. He's scared.

The blue vase falls from his hands.

I am not ugly!

Clunk jumps and catches the vase.

'I have it!' he says.

'Let's go!' says the man with the flashlight.

The two robbers run. They want to go to the window. But they can hear police cars in the street.

→ Go to page 26 for activities.

Grandpa and Bill are at the door. There are some police officers with them.

Bill points at the two robbers. 'There!' he says.

'Stop!' shouts a police officer to the robbers.

Stop!

Clunk gives the vase to Bill.

'Thank you,' says Bill. 'This vase is very old.'

'Let's go home, Grandpa,' says Rosie. 'I want to paint my picture now!'

 Go to page 27 for activities.

1 Write the words.

1 t ᵃ c

2 c ᵗ u e r p i

3 c w ₒ

cat

_____

_____

4 a ⁱ n t p

5 r ᵉ s h o

6 t r ₐ

_____

_____

_____

2 Write *yes* or *no*.

1 Rosie is painting at the table. ___yes___

2 Ben is painting a picture, too. _____

3 Rosie paints a horse. _____

4 Rosie paints a cat. _____

5 Rosie says, 'I'm not good at art.' _____

Talk **Do you like painting? Talk to a friend.**

Activities for pages 6-7

1 Circle the correct words.

1 '**Do** / **Are** you want to go to the art museum?'

2 Grandpa's friend Bill **are** / **is** a guard.

3 Grandpa wants **giving** / **to give** Bill a book.

4 Clunk drives the van **to** / **at** the museum.

5 Grandpa sees **his** / **him** friend Bill.

6 'Nice to **meet** / **meeting** you!'

2 Put a tick (✓) or a cross (✗) in the box.

1 This is a guard. ✗

2 This is a museum.

3 This is a robot. ⬜

4 These are children.

Activities for pages 8-9

1 Choose and write the correct words.

Grandpa and Bill talk about the ¹ _____book_____.

Ben, Rosie, and Clunk look at the ² _____.

Ben ³ _____ at a blue vase. Clunk doesn't

like the ⁴ _____. They look at the statues.

Clunk doesn't like the statues.

points   statue   museum   ~~book~~   vase

2 Complete the sentences.

> points ~~talk~~ look goes like

1 Bill wants to _____talk_____ to Grandpa.

2 'You can _____ at the museum.'

3 Clunk _____ with Ben and Rosie.

4 'Do you _____ art, Clunk?'

5 Ben _____ at a blue vase.

Talk **Do you like art? Talk to a friend.**

Activities for pages 10–11

1 Order the words.

1 likes / colors / a picture. / Ben / in / the

  Ben likes the colors in a picture.

2 likes / sign! / Clunk / a / museum

  _____

3 and Rosie / hear / people. / Ben / can

  _____

4 points / window. / Ben / a / at

  _____

5 the window. / There's / man / a / at

  _____

2 Look at the picture on page 10. Write *yes* or *no*.

1 There are three pictures. _____no_____

2 Rosie is looking at a picture. _____

3 Clunk is looking at a sign. _____

4 Ben is talking to Grandpa. _____

5 Clunk has a vase. _____

6 There is a window. _____

Activities for pages 12–13

1 Write the words.

steal   move   ~~clothes~~   idea

1    **2**    **3**    **4**

clothes   _____   _____   _____

2 Order the words.

1 want to / Two / the art. / men / steal

_____

2 a door / There / the children. / isn't / close to

_____

3 stand / next / They / to / the statues.

_____

4 move. / talk / and don't / Now don't

_____

Talk **Do the men see Ben, Rosie, and Clunk? Tell a friend your ideas.**

Activities for pages 14–15

1 Choose and write the correct words.

The two robbers are in the museum now.
One ¹ _____ has the blue vase. One
robber has a ² _____. He looks at some
pictures. The robber with the vase wants to
steal a ³ _____. The robbers look at the
⁴ _____ and Clunk.

flashlight   statue   robber   children   vase

2 Match. Then write the sentences.

1 'What do you   •   • steal a statue.'

2 'I want to   •   • this little statue.'

3 'I don't like   •   • want to steal?'

1   *'What do you want to steal?'*

2 _____

3 _____

Activities for pages 16–17

1 Write the words.

1 l k a t

_____

2 h a d n s

_____

3 u m j p

_____

4 a f l l

_____

5 c s r a e d

_____

6 c a h t c

_____

2 Look at the big picture on page 16. Write *yes* or *no*.

1 Clunk is next to Rosie. _____

2 One robber has a flashlight. _____

3 One robber has a statue. _____

4 Clunk is talking. _____

5 The robbers' clothes are black. _____

Activities for pages 18-19

1 Circle the correct words.

1 Grandpa is **with** / **at** some police officers.

2 Bill points at the **two** / **too** robbers.

3 A police officer **shouting** / **shouts**, 'Stop!'

4 Clunk **gives** / **give** the vase to Bill.

5 Rosie wants **painting** / **to paint** her picture.

2 Put a tick (✓) or a cross (✗) in the box.

 1 This is a door. ☐

 2 This is a police officer. ☐

 3 This is a robber. ☐

 4 This is a police car. ☐

Talk **Do you like this story? Talk to a friend.**

Talk about Art!

1 Complete the chart.

cat   vase   horse   black   museum   red
statue   blue   cow   picture   bird   green

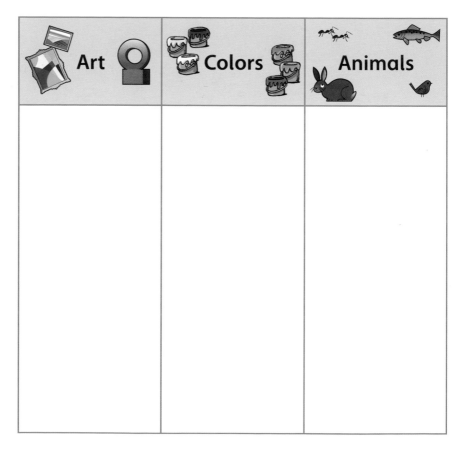

Art	Colors	Animals

2 Do you know more art, color, and animal words? Write them in the chart.

3 Look at the picture and answer the questions.

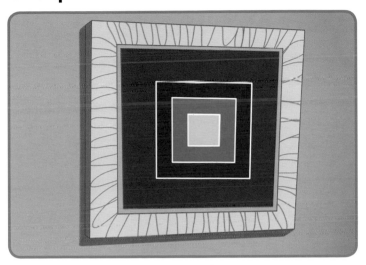

What can you see?

What colors can you see?

Do you like the colors?

Is it a happy picture or a sad picture?

Do you like the picture?

Talk **Talk to a friend about the picture.**

Picture Dictionary

art

cat

catch

children

clothes

cow

fall

flashlight

guard

horse

idea

meet

move

museum

paint

people

 picture

 point

 police car

 police officer

 robber

 robot

 scared

 shout

 sign

 statue

 steal

 stop

 street

 van

 vase

 window

Oxford Read and Imagine

Oxford Read and Imagine graded readers are at eight levels (Starter, Beginner, and Levels 1 to 6) for students from age 4 and older. They offer great stories to read and enjoy.

Activities provide Cambridge Young Learner Exams preparation. See Key below.

At Levels 1 to 6, every storybook reader links to an **Oxford Read and Discover** non-fiction reader, giving students a chance to find out more about the world around them, and an opportunity for Content and Language Integrated Learning (CLIL).

For more information about **Read and Imagine**, and for Teacher's Notes, go to www.oup.com/elt/teacher/readandimagine

KEY Activity supports Cambridge Young Learners Starters Exam preparation

 Oxford Read and Discover

Do you want to find out more about art and art museums?
You can read this non-fiction book.

OXFORD
UNIVERSITY PRESS

Great Clarendon Street, Oxford, OX2 6DP, United Kingdom

Oxford University Press is a department of the University of Oxford. It furthers the University's objective of excellence in research, scholarship, and education by publishing worldwide. Oxford is a registered trade mark of Oxford University Press in the UK and in certain other countries

ISBN: 978 0 19 472270 4

Printed in China

This book is printed on paper from certified and well-managed sources

ACKNOWLEDGEMENTS

Main illustrations by: Fabiano Fiorin/Milan Illustrations Agency.

Activity illustrations by: Dusan Pavlic/Beehive Illustration; Alan Rowe; Mark Ruffle.